Santa Fe

the city different

Text by
Justine Thomas
~
Photographs by
David King

the sunstone press
Santa Fe, New Mexico / 1973

FIRST EDITION

ISBN 0 – 913270 – 21 – 0

Printed in the United States of America
Printed by Starline, Albuquerque, New Mexico

**We dedicate this to all
who love Santa Fe as we do.**

BRIEFLY – – – HISTORY

La Villa Real de Santa Fe de San Francisco de Assisi, the Royal City of the Holy Faith of Saint Francis of Assisi, was founded in 1610 as the capital of the northern portion of New Spain. Don Juan de Oñate in 1598 had established a Spanish settlement and capital near San Juan Pueblo about 30 miles northwest of Santa Fe. Twelve years later, Don Pedro de Peralta moved the capital to its present location on the site of an ancient Indian pueblo ruin. The city was laid out from a design by King Phillip II, of Spain.

Santa Fe is the highest capital city in the United States, being at an elevation of 7,000 feet; the oldest capital, dating from 1610, and the only one without a major railroad or large industry. The 1970 census placed the population at 41,000.

The city has been a capital under six governments:

1610 – 1680	Capital of the Northern Kingdom of New Spain.
1680 – 1693	The Pueblo Indians revolted against the Spanish in 1680 and held the city until 1693.
1693 – 1821	After the bloodless reconquest of the city from the Pueblo Indians by General Don Diego de Vargas, the province returned to Spanish rule.
1821 – 1822	The Empire of Mexico claimed the territory that had belonged to Spain.
1822 – 1846	In 1822, Mexico became a Republic and sent her governors and emissaries to the north.
1846 – 1912	General Stephen Watts Kearny took the city from the Mexican forces in 1846 and the United States Territory of New Mexico came into being.
1862	For about a month the Confederate Army controlled the city until their defeat at the Battle of Glorieta Pass.
1912	The Territory of New Mexico became the 47th State.

The town sits in a saucer-like valley surrounded by the Sangre de Cristo Mountains on the north and northeast (with peaks up to 13,300 ft.), the Ortiz Mountains to the southeast, the Sandias on the south and the Jemez range on the west.

Within a few miles is the Pueblo Indian country, archeological ruins and ghost towns. The nearby mountains provide beautiful camping and hiking areas, wonderful fishing and in the winter, marvelous skiing.

The new State Capital Executive Building is an architecturally stylized version of the Zia Sun Symbol which also appears on the State flag. The doors are of bronze and are inlaid with turquoise. The other buildings in the Capital complex are in what is called the Territorial style.

The center of all town activity was and still is the Plaza. Once, long ago, during weekdays it teemed with the bustle of a busy marketplace, but on Sunday evenings, that was changed. The Plaza became a Promenade and the *Dueñas* (chaperons) and their young ladies took over. To the music of the band concert on the bandstand the ladies strolled in one direction around the Plaza and the young gentlemen walked in the opposite direction. In 1821 William Becknell brought in the first wagonload of goods from the East, thus opening the Santa Fe Trail. A marker at the southeast corner marks the end of the Santa Fe Trail. The tall obelisk in the center honors Civil War heroes.

Today, as yesterday, all parades and processions go around the Plaza. Public functions, speakers and visiting dignitaries are presented on the grandstand. The main activities of the Fiesta take place here.

The Plaza was declared a National Historic Landmark by the United States Government in 1962.

El Palacio Real, the Palace of the Governors, is the oldest government building in the United States, having been used for this purpose from 1610 to 1912 under six governments. Built of thick adobe as the fortress headquarters for the Northern Kingdom of New Spain, it was all that remained of the city after the Pueblo Revolt of 1680. It became a Museum in 1909 and today houses archeological and historical exhibits of New Mexico and the Southwest.

It was here that General Lew Wallace, when he was Territorial Governor, finished his magnificent book *Ben Hur.* In addition to housing the government offices, *El Palacio* served as the governor's residence and many gala *bailes* and parties were held here.

The Indians from the nearby pueblos gather under the Portal every day to display and sell their handcrafted jewelry and other articles. Try some of their bread or prune pie – it is delicious.

The Fine Arts Museum, known locally as the New Museum, was dedicated on November 25, 1917 to house the Art of the Southwest and other Fine Art Exhibits. It is a replica of the New Mexico Building built in San Diego for the Panama-California Exposition in 1913. The design incorporates some exterior features of the Mission Churches at San Felipe and Cochiti Pueblos. The locks on the two doors are handmade from colonial days and the bell is an old one cast in Spain centuries ago.

When excavating for the foundations, the ruins of an ancient pueblo were uncovered.

St. Francis Auditorium at the west end of the Fine Arts Museum is a copy of the Mission Church at Acoma Pueblo. A very fine pipe organ is housed here and many musical concerts are presented in the auditorium. The auditorium seats 678. The beautiful murals of the life of St. Francis were painted by Donald Beauregard, Carlos Vierra and Kenneth Chapman.

The picture above is of an old home built in 1864 for his bride by Don José D. Sena. Now called Sena Plaza, it houses shops and offices. The walls, roofs, most of the doors and windows are the original ones. The second floor on the west was the Sala Grande, the Ballroom. Behind the home was a large orchard and stables.

The beautiful patio in Sena Plaza was the center of the family life. Don José and his wife had twenty-three children, so one can easily imagine the playing and laughter that these walls echoed.

The Federal Building across from the Cathedral is still called by Santa Feans the Old Post Office. Note the lovely carved corbels and *vigas* of the portal and the beautiful Santa Fe Style architecture. Truly it was one of the most beautiful Post Offices in the U.S.A.

The portal showing the carved corbels and *vigas.*

Saint Francis Cathedral was begun by Archbishop Lamy in 1869 on the site of a Church and Convent built in 1626 at the eastern end of San Francisco street. At that time the Plaza extended to the front of the Church. Stone workers from Italy were brought here by the Archbishop to work the native stone. The towers have never been completed.

The legend is that the Hebrew inscription over the main entrance is in honor of the local Jewish merchants who helped finance the building.

Our Lady of the Conquest, a beautiful statue carried by the armies of De Vargas over 300 years ago, has her special Chapel to the right of the main altar. La Conquistadora, as she is lovingly called, is taken each year from the Cathedral to Rosario Chapel and back to start the annual Fiesta.

Recently the interior of the Church was remodeled and the many beautiful old statues and carvings, including the great high altar, were removed to give a more modern decor.

The city is divided north to south by the Santa Fe River. Recently the banks have been landscaped into pleasant and beautiful parks. Don't be deceived by the small amount or lack of running water. Many times, and as recent as six years ago, the river has overflowed its banks and bridges. All that is needed is a heavy rain in the mountains to the east. Travelers should also note that any and all dry arroyos can be extremely dangerous being subject to walls of water flowing swiftly following heavy rain in the nearby mountains.

Two of the oldest streets are Canyon Road and Acequia Madre. Canyon Road, now a street of many arts and crafts shops, was used by the woodcutters and their burros to bring wood into town from the hills southeast of the city. What fun it was to buy a load of piñon wood, packed high and round, off the burrito's back.

The Acequia Madre (Mother Ditch) was the main irrigation ditch for the homes and gardens on the south side of the river. Our water comes from Santa Fe Canyon and was routed over the city by a series of acequias. Because much of this water went to the State Penitentiary, every spring a trustee on horseback traveled along the ditch and cleaned the winter's debris. Each section had a water master (Mayordomo) who saw that the ditch was kept clean and flowing and that each person received his share of water. Water has always been very precious here and family water rights are most important. The position of Mayordomo is very highly regarded.

Santa Fe Street Scene

Cristo Rey Church, the largest adobe structure in the United States was completed in 1939 to house the lovely stone reredos. This hand-carved stone altar screen was found behind a wall of the Cathedral and had come from a much older Church on the south side of the Plaza. Be sure to notice the beautiful ceiling.

The Mission of San Miguel is the oldest church in the United States, having been built for the use of soldiers and servants of New Spain. According to Fra Alonso de Benavides, by 1626 the Chapel had already been in use for quite some time.

The Church of Our Lady of Guadalupe was built in 1795 and named for the patron saint of both Old and New Mexico.

Across from San Miguel Mission in the area called *Barrio Del Analco* is what many consider the oldest house in the United States. The foundation and lower walls are very old Indian construction, being puddled adobe, a method predating brick adobe. This was the area where the soldiers lived during the Spanish occupancy.

Pictured above is the lovely and beautiful Chapel of Our Lady of Light, built in 1874-78 and called Loretto Chapel. Until 1970 the Sisters of Loretto had a convent and school on these grounds. Inside is the "Miraculous Staircase," built in a spiral without nails or supports.

Santa Fe Style Architecture is unique, being a blend of Spanish and Pueblo. Many of the homes and buildings, both old and new, are built of adobe or are in adobe style. Modern subdivisions are in "Adobe Style," constructed of pumice or concrete block or frame stucco. Adobe is great insulation, keeping a building cool in the summer and retaining heat for warmth in winter. The Historic Santa Fe Foundation and the Old Santa Fe Association are hard-working, active groups involved in keeping and restoring the city's old buildings and thereby retaining its charm.

The Inn At The End Of The Santa Fe Trail – La Fonda

The Borrego House – Now A Coffee House

The Delgado House – An Office Building

Padre Gallegos House — Office Building

The religious fervency that inspired the exploration and colonization by the Spanish Conquistadores still is very much a part of Santa Fe. For most of her life Santa Fe has been predominately Roman Catholic. This has changed some with the increase of newcomers since World War II. At the present time there are:

5 Roman Catholic Churches
26 Protestant Churches
1 Jewish Temple
as well as
Church of Christ Scientist
Seventh Day Adventist
Latter-Day Saints
Bahai
Unitarian Fellowship
Society of Friends

Many have been built in Santa Fe Style.

Presbyterian Church
Temple Beth Shalom
First Church of Christ Scientist
First Baptist Church

TEMPLE
BETH SHALOM
205

FIRST CHURCH OF CHRIST, SCIENTIST
FIRST CHURCH OF CHRIST SCIENTIST
SANTA FE, NEW MEXICO

In the mid-1800's the Christian Brothers started a school for boys, elementary through high school called St. Michael's. In 1949 the Brothers founded St. Michael's College, an accredited four-year college, now co-educational and called The College of Santa Fe. Present enrollment is 1,200.

Santa Fe is noted for its cosmopolitan atmosphere because of its many artists and authors. The city enjoys ballet, concerts, symphonies, the famed Santa Fe Opera and many theatrical groups. The School of American Research is located here and yearly, archeologists and anthropologists from around the world gather for seminars. There are two four-year colleges.

In 1964 St. John's College of Annapolis, Maryland, opened a branch college here in Santa Fe. St. John's is one of the oldest liberal arts institutions in the United States. Present enrollment is 260.

The charm that is Santa Fe is partly the homes of adobe with their soft lines, walled patios and *placitas.* Even if it was built yesterday and furnished with the most modern furniture, outside the house presents a serene and private atmosphere. We are a city of trees, bright flowers and in the spring, the lilacs are outstandingly beautiful.

NIELSEN ART
GALLERY
701

Ammunition storage house built during the Civil War of native stone.

Santa Fe is a fortunate place because of the blending of three major cultures – Indian, Spanish-Mexican and Anglo. Above is an example of an all Anglo building and on the next page is an example of purely Indian. Most Santa Fe architecture shows Pueblo Indian influence; the Museum of Navaho Ceremonial Art is built as an eight-sided hogan. At one time all Navaho homes were built in that form.

Museum of Navaho Ceremonial Art.

VIVA LA FIESTA

Started in 1712, the Santa Fe Fiesta has been celebrated ever since that time. Over Labor Day weekend, Santa Fe relaxes, has fun, and honors the memory of the bloodless reconquest of the city by General Don Diego de Vargas. Special homage goes to La Conquistadora, the little statue in the Cathedral who guided De Vargas and led him to victory. Fiesta has changed over the years, but music, dancing and fun are still the main activities. Zozobra (Old Man Gloom) is burned on Friday night and laughter and happiness reign. On the Plaza there is singing and dancing. Strolling musicians and Mariachi Bands play all day and most of the night. On Saturday is the *Desfile de Los Niños,* or Pet Parade. All the children and most of the pets are in costume.

JUSTINE D. THOMAS was born in Santa Fe, New Mexico and attended school there until the tenth grade. At that time she moved to Pasadena, California. She graduated from Pasadena Junior College. In 1949, she and her family returned to Santa Fe and moved into the house her grandfather had built in 1911. Mrs. Thomas is the mother of two married daughters and has two grandchildren. Since 1966 she has owned the Villagrá Book Shop located in historic Sena Plaza.

DAVID KING of San Diego, California is a free-lance photographer. He attended the University of Denver, Colorado State University and Kansas City Art Institute. A former teacher of photography and news photographer, Mr. King is presently attending Western State University College of Law. He served in the Armed Forces from 1966-1970 as an Information Specialist.